Crossing the Bridges God Builds

Gary A. Burlingame

Outreach can be simple!

In this book, Gary Burlingame leads us in a discovery of how the simple things, done with compassion and love, make a big difference in the lives of our neighbors. This is a great resource for personal reflection, or family and small group discussion.

Eric Wallace
President
Uniting Church and Home

CROSSING THE BRIDGES GOD BUILDS
Copyright © 2015 by Gary A. Burlingame

Published by:
Healthy Life Press • 9375 Blue Mountain Drive • Golden, CO 80403
www.healthylifepress.com

Author: Gary A. Burlingame
Designer: Judy Johnson

Printed in the United States of America

No part of this publication may be reproduced, stored in a retrieval system, or transmitted in any form or by any means—for example, electronic, photocopy, recording—without the prior written permission of the author, except for brief quotations in printed reviews.

Library of Congress Cataloging-in-Publication Data
Burlingame, Gary A.
Crossing the Bridges God Builds

ISBN **978-1-939267-07-8**

1. RELIGION / Christian Ministry / Evangelism
2. RELIGION / Christian Ministry / Pastoral Resources

Scripture quotes taken from:

New International Version
The Holy Bible, New International Version
Copyright © 1973, 1978, 1984 by the International Bible Society
All Rights Reserved

Most Healthy Life Press resources are available wherever books are sold. Distribution is primarily through www.Amazon.com, www.deepershopping.com, and www.healthylifepress.com. Multiple copy discounts available directly from Healthy Life Press. Wholesale distribution is through www.SpringArbor.com (a division of www.IngramContent.com), and www.deepershopping.com. Our ePublications are available through www.healthylifepress.com, www.Amazon.com (Kindle), www.BN.com (Nook), and for all eBook readers through www.deepershopping.com. Wholesale copies of our eBooks are also available through www.IngramContent.com (www.SpringArbor.com). Combination offers of printed and electronic books of the same title are available at a discount from the publisher at: www.healthylifepress.com. Resources ordered directly from the publisher receive free shipping. For information on our products, or how to publish with us, e-mail: info@healthylifepress.com.

The opinions expressed in this book are those of the author and/or any other contributors and may not represent the official position of Healthy Life Press, its publisher, or any of its other authors.

Contents

Stay, Don't Go	1
God is a Bridge Builder	4
We are Called to Cross the Bridges	7
Recognizing the Existing Bridges	14
The Primary Bridge is to Family Members	19
The Secondary Bridge Includes our Family of Faith	22
Two Ends of a Bridge—One Anchored in Households	25
The Role of Leadership	30
Take Home Message	37
References and Additional Reading	39

Stay, Don't Go!

It was Monday morning. I caught the bus to work. I barely noticed people around me because I was preoccupied. My mind was still buzzing from my pastor's sermon.

> "Go to Africa. Go build a church in Appalachia. Go into the city and feed the homeless. Go, go, go!"

> I was so focused on where I should "Go" that I walked right past my neighbor who was fixing a flat tire. I ignored the elderly woman who couldn't run fast enough to catch the bus when I got on. I overlooked the teenager who had attended elementary school with my daughter. I was so engrossed with *going* that I lost sight of *staying* and the opportunities that God provides right in my own backyard.

Whether we feel compelled to go or content to stay, we are called to love our neighbors. Monte Swan and David Biebel, authors of *Romancing Your Child's Heart*, reminded us that; "We were made by Love and for love. We don't love God because we must, but because 'He first loved us' (John 1:4-19)." The directive to *love* comes from the Lord (Mark 12:28-31):

> "Of all the commandments, which is the most important?" "The most important one," answered Jesus, "is this: 'Hear, O Israel, the Lord our God, the Lord is one. Love the Lord your God with all your heart and with all your soul and with all your mind and with all your strength.' The second is this: 'Love your neighbor as yourself.' There is no commandment greater than these."

A middle-aged, single woman wanted to serve in the church and she felt guilty for not being active in a ministry. I asked her to think of ways she could help that would bring joy to her. She desired to help parents with their babies. So we came up with a way for her to do this; during the worship service she would hold and care for a baby to make it easier for the mom to worship and focus on the sermon. That was a start. She began helping her neighbors in her church. Once again, we sometimes overlook the obvious—the opportunities to serve people right where we are, using our existing skills.

Study Questions

1. What activities have you been involved with in your community?

2. How did you get involved in these activities?

3. Have you ever helped someone get connected into a community? If you did, how?

4. Have you ever felt overwhelmed by the needs of someone you met in your community?

5. Is there a local community activity that you have had a desire to become a part of but have not yet had a chance to participate in?

God is a Bridge Builder

The Bible tells the story of community—community created, fallen, re-built, redeemed, and yet to come. Sin brought alienation into that community. At the Tower of Babel (Genesis 11:1-9), God separated the growing community by sending different peoples out to form different nations. Then in Genesis 12-17, God brought back together His covenant community through Abraham. In the New Testament, Christ came to redeem His community of Jews and Gentiles. Today, God's community is being reconciled, redeemed, and healed because Christ now lives among His people (1 Peter 2:9-10). Therefore, community is where we belong.

The image of a bridge is a useful image to consider when studying God's community. Bridges connect people. They allow people to come and go across barriers or gaps that would otherwise separate them. A bridge can be small and easily crossed, or long and wide. It can be for crossing one at a time, or it can be a bustling center of two-way traffic. Some are rickety while others can withstand raging waters and strong winds. Some were built by one person; others by multiple groups of specialized craftsmen. The many ways in which we have established various kinds of relationships with other people are our bridges. They might be a shared experience, a common interest, a shared necessity, a personal relationship, a business transaction, a habit, a hobby, or a preference. They might be the need to have a car inspected every year, the schools we take our children to, the corner markets where we shop, being summoned to jury duty, sharing food with a local homeless person, or our places of work.

God is a bridge builder. He is connecting people. We should expect that He will give us bridges to cross. If we truly believe that God is sovereign, then we should expect Him to connect us to the people He is calling us to love. And in creating those connections, God uses us as we are and where we are; even in our frailty and weakness. Sometimes we stand up as a leader, an example of courage and strength. Other times we connect with people who are hurting and in pain, or who feel lost. Sometimes it happens when our children score the winning goal in a soccer game. Sometimes it happens when we are afraid, as in an emergency room, or when we are deep in grief at a funeral home. God weaves all of this together—the bridge building; our mental, emotional, and spiritual condition; our circumstances—to place us in the right place at the right time to love our neighbors.

Study Questions

1. What bridges, or ways to connect with people, did the Apostles build during their ministries? How were everyday people a part of those bridges?

2. Describe the neighborhood in which you live. Where might bridges already exist?

3. Can you share some examples of bridges that others have crossed to get into your life?

4. Describe some of the challenges that your community is facing today. How might any one of those challenges create a bridge for building new relationships?

We are Called to Cross the Bridges

Timothy Keller, who is a recognized author, speaker, and pastor of Redeemer Presbyterian Church in Manhattan, wrote that; "Mercy to the full range of human needs is such an essential mark of being a Christian that it can be used as a test of true faith. Mercy is not optional or an addition to being a Christian. Rather, a life poured out in deeds of mercy is the inevitable sign of true faith." Mercy is part of God's plan:

> Micah 6:8 – He has showed you, O man, what is good. And what does the Lord require of you? To act justly and to love mercy and to walk humbly with your God.

> Ephesians 2:4-5 – But because of His great love for us, God, who is rich in mercy, made us alive with Christ even when we were dead in transgressions—it is by grace you have been saved.

Mercy has two aspects to it: first, the showing of compassion; second, the withholding of judgment (James 2:12-13). Compassion is often our response to felt needs. Jesus looked out upon the crowds of people following him and showed compassion (Matthew 14:14; 15:32; 20:34; Mark 1:41; 6:34). The Bible compels us to show compassion:

Psalm 41:1 – Blessed is he who has regard for the weak; the Lord delivers him in times of trouble.

Psalm 82:3 – Defend the cause of the weak and fatherless; maintain the right of the poor and oppressed.

Isaiah 58:6-7 – Is not this the kind of fasting I have chosen: to loose the chains of injustice and untie the cords of the yoke, to set the oppressed free and break every yoke? Is it not to share your food with the hungry, and to provide the poor wanderer with shelter—when you see the naked, to clothe him, and not to turn away from your own flesh and blood?

Keller stated that in the establishment of the office of deacons; "This shows that mercy is a mandated work of the church, just as are the ministry of the Word and discipline." Keller went on to state that; "The striking truth is that the work of mercy is fundamental to being a Christian." Unfortunately, the ministry of mercy or compassion has often been left in the laps of the deacons, or placed lower on the priority list of church activities, or even neglected.

Fortunately, there are very basic ways we can practice compassion in everyday life. Listening, for example, is a powerful witness in a self-focused culture. Listening helps create a safe place where someone can express fears, guilt, shame, grief, or issues of the heart. Listening can help build trust. It requires that we forget ourselves and put our interests aside. In an everyday sense, loving our neighbors is done by listening to and caring for the people around us.

Compassion or empathy for the one who is suffering along with a desire to alleviate the suffering can be an awesome tool used by the Spirit of God to soften the hearts of our neighbors to the Gospel wherein is found the mercy of Christ. Mark Gornik, who is the director of City Seminary of New York, stated it this way; "When people know they are deeply loved, cared for, accepted, and wanted by a community, they are transformed by the experience." Keller simplified this truth by writing; "Mercy has an impact. It melts hearts. It removes objections."

Gornik reminds us that; "When we speak of the church of the poor and suffering, one that is evangelical in the gospel sense, it is important to emphasize that we do not mean a church that has a unique concern or special ministry to the poor, a mission from the outside. Rather, a church of the poor is a fellowship amidst the hurting and harmed, the excluded and the suffering."

God has engulfed our lives in relationships. These relationships are the *existing* bridges to the neighbors we are called to love. We must cross these bridges to our neighbors. And we need compassion as we cross them so that we reflect God's heart for the people on the other end.

Take a moment and reflect on the various ways in which you have helped different people. In so doing you will increase your awareness of opportunities for mercy ministry in everyday life. You might be surprised with what you have already been doing. Consider the parable of the Good Samaritan and how a businessman creatively used his resources to help a stranger:

> Luke 10:34-37 – He went to him and bandaged his wounds, pouring oil and wine. Then he put the man on his own donkey, took him to an inn and took care of him.

In Luke we find several examples of how Jesus met the obvious felt needs of the people around him:

> Luke 4:38-39 – Jesus healed a woman with high fever
> Luke 5:12-13 – Jesus cured a man with leprosy
> Luke 8:40-48 – Jesus healed a bleeding woman
> Luke 8:49-56 – Jesus brought a girl back to life

Examples of Opportunities in Everyday Life

What Did You Do?	Who Did You Help?					
	Close and Personal Neighbor			Common Neighbor	Occasional Neighbor
	Relative	Close Friend	Church Family	Someone You See Often	Stranger Someone You See Infrequently
1. Gave a bus token to a stranger					X
2. Gave food to a homeless person					X
3. Treated a co-worker to lunch				X	
4. Shoveled snow for a neighbor				X	
5. Visited a co-worker in the hospital				X	
6. Raised funds at work for a co-worker's med. expenses				X	
7. Gave someone a ride home from church			X		
8. Provided encouragement and advice			X		
9. Coached someone with their personal budget			X		
10. Had a friend over for dinner		X			
11. Offered a listening ear	X				
12. Picked up groceries for grandparents	X				

Thus, God has placed us where He can use us. In this place we develop bridges to our neighbors. In this place we are called to use our existing skills and resources to meet the obvious or felt needs of our neighbors. And in meeting the obvious felt needs of our neighbors we open up opportunity to:

- Reveal deeper spiritual needs
- Share the love of Christ
- Declare the Good News.

Our communities contain households, which are quite varied: a household could be a single adult; a couple of young men sharing a house together; a complete family; a single parent; a widow or widower, and so on. All of these varied households need to see themselves as the building blocks of their communities, out of which mercy and love can radiate. The uniqueness of each household feeds into the creative ways in which loving our neighbors can take place, as arranged by our sovereign God.

Study Questions

1. Describe some ways in which you have received compassion from someone else.

2. Is the act of loving your neighbor always an easy way to serve the Lord? Why? Why not?

3. Share some ways in which it has been difficult to love your neighbor.

4. How have your own attitudes made it difficult to respond in love to the needs of a neighbor?

5. Have you ever missed an opportunity to help someone? Explain.

6. See if you can fill out the form on the right using your own experiences.

Examples of Opportunities in Everyday Life

What Did You Do?	Who Did You Help?			
	Close and Personal Neighbor			Common Neighbor	Occasional Neighbor
	Relative	Close Friend	Church Family	Someone You See Often	Stranger Someone You See Infrequently
1					
2					
3					
4					
5					
6					
7					
8					
9					
10					
11					
12					

Recognizing the Existing Bridges

God created Man in His image. Man and woman He created in His image, to propagate and fill the earth with neighbors, family by family. Our relationship with God as well as with each other demonstrates God's design for the relationships we have here on earth and with Him. Swan and Biebel summarized the need we have as individuals for each other; "We find our temporal and eternal identity, purpose, and fulfillment in relationship, with God and with others. Relationship is the web of meaning that connects all the components of our lives, enabling us to be whole physically and spiritually."

God has created us for, and called us into community. Community is where we proclaim the Good News, repent, forgive, reconcile, baptize, teach, fellowship, praise, worship, and love one another (Acts 2:42-47; Acts 4:32-35). The spiritual gifts we are given—such as for serving, teaching, encouraging, giving and leading (Romans 12:3-8)—are designed for community. As the body of Christ, we live in community. This community is comprised of relationships woven together to form a community of mutual interdependence. The bricks that build community, our relationships, are not placed happenstance. The Spirit of God is at work.

But who are our neighbors? Neighbors vary from household to

household because relationships vary. Some people have friends they have known since childhood. Others have relocated so frequently that they have not had the opportunity to sustain long-term friendships. Some people have relatives—aunts, uncles, cousins, grandparents, nieces and nephews—that live close by. Some people live in row homes, some live in single homes, some on farms, and some live in apartments. Some work a full-time job, some attend school, some are retired, and some are homemakers. How do all these people get connected? Perhaps they get connected through life-long relationships. Perhaps by working together, volunteering in community programs, or attending a church. Perhaps they come together when their children play together. Or some people may connect simply by saying "Hello" to each other every day.

Consider our relationships as the three sections of a tree: the outer bark; the thicker inner section; and the innermost core:

- The **outer bark of relationships** comprises our co-workers, schoolmates, and peers. Also included are the people we meet occasionally such as store owners, car mechanics, plumbers, doctors, and teachers. We don't usually have direct responsibility for, or experience close accountability with these people. Though this layer of relationships is most apparent, it should not be what defines us. The bark will shed, peel, even come off completely: sometimes forced off by inner growth and sometimes pulled off by outside pressure.

- The **middle or inner ring of relationships** is the support group of close friends, spouse, brother and sister, and church family. Though the outer bark be peeled off, if it reveals a solid inner structure then healthy growth will reform the bark again. Healthy bark depends on this inner layer. Also, this layer shows the rings of time and maturity. Years of good watering, such as with the Spirit's leading, show thick rings. Years of drought, such as without the Spirit's leading, form thin rings. Our more intimate relationships indeed go through times of abundance and times of drought.

Relationships:
Consider the Three Sections of a Tree

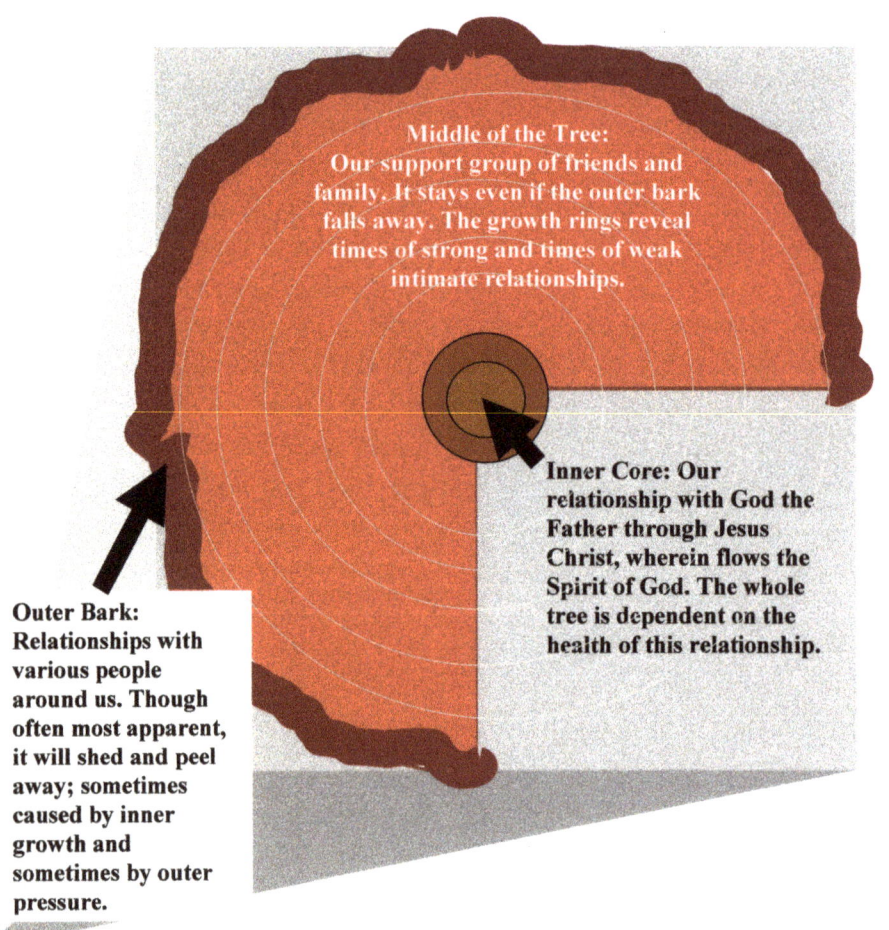

Middle of the Tree: Our support group of friends and family. It stays even if the outer bark falls away. The growth rings reveal times of strong and times of weak intimate relationships.

Inner Core: Our relationship with God the Father through Jesus Christ, wherein flows the Spirit of God. The whole tree is dependent on the health of this relationship.

Outer Bark: Relationships with various people around us. Though often most apparent, it will shed and peel away; sometimes caused by inner growth and sometimes by outer pressure.

- The **innermost core** is our relationship with Jesus Christ. The Spirit of God carries the life force through the core, coming from the roots grounded in the love and mercy of the Father who provides the nourishment for our growth. The abundance of fruit on the branches arises from the flow of the Spirit through the core. The crown of branches depends on the strength and stability of the roots, on how well they are grounded in the truth and love of the Father. If this core rots, though not evident by the bark, the tree will not stand for long.

The Bible describes God's plan for Christian community, with Jesus as the community developer. Jesus re-creates us in community with God and with each other, and His teachings provide the principles for living under the broad umbrella of *loving God* and *loving others*. Community is strengthened, and will grow and mature through the giving and receiving of sacrificial love in healthy and constructive ways.

God does not call us to love others in isolation or by our own strength. God sets us up with complementary skills and capabilities so that by working together we can better meet the needs of our neighbors. In addition, we need to be in communication with each other so that the care and love we provide is constructive and coordinated. This is especially important, knowing that we live in a sinful world, where our neighbors will, at times, manipulate us to get what they want, when they want it. Thus, when we take up the call to love our neighbors, it is best to approach that call, as appropriate, in teams. Working together, we have prayer partners, second opinions, and someone to hold us accountable. And we have someone to share the experience with; the ups and downs, the frustrations, and the celebrations. This is what community is all about!

Study Questions

1. Make a list of the people who comprise the "outer bark" of relationships in your life today. Estimate how many of these people have known you for ten years or more. Do you consider your "outer bark" to be shedding or growing thicker?

2. Make a list of the people who comprise the "rings of your tree" in your life today. How healthy is this layer of relationships? Are you currently experiencing a time of drought or of abundance with regards to the spiritual aspects of these inner relationships?

3. How healthy is your "innermost core" today? Please explain.

The Primary Bridge is to Family Members

Our first responsibility in meeting felt needs lies with our own families and households. In 1 Timothy 5:8 we read: "If anyone does not provide for his relatives, and especially for his immediate family, he has denied the faith and is worse than an unbeliever."

Sometimes we don't realize that our own habits steal care away from our own families. I remember a situation where a mother's spending diverted money away from caring for her own children, causing her to request more assistance from the church which in turn reduced the church's ability to provide help to others:

> We sat on the sofa. She brought us iced tea. The children watched TV.
>
> "Thank you for the tea. How can we help and pray for you? Being a single mom must be difficult."
>
> "I need food money. Everything else is okay."
>
> "I think I saw that TV show once when my family was staying at a hotel on vacation. Is that on cable TV?"

"Yes, my children watch many shows on cable TV."

"And I guess you like to read. There are a lot of magazines on the table."

"I guess that's my weakness. I subscribe to about twelve magazines. But I also give to Christian ministries."

"So, how much do you estimate you could use a month for food money?"

"Well, I had to borrow 25 dollars last week from a friend. So maybe about 100 dollars a month. I do give to church. I gave 15 dollars last Sunday."

"In my own life, I have found ways to increase my income by reducing how much I spend such as by not going out to eat at fast-food restaurants. Are there any ways that you can reduce your spending? How about we pray before you answer? Let's get our hearts on the right track before we try to solve any problems."

Study Questions

1. Read 1 Timothy 5:8. What does the "provision" include that we must provide to our families?

2. Why is helping family members sometimes difficult?

3. What constitutes a family's essential needs? How do you think that non-essential needs sometimes confuse the provision of help? For example, is having a cell phone an essential need? What type of phone would be essential?

4. Describe some creative ways in which your household can help other families.

5. Describe some creative ways in which your church can help families.

The Secondary Bridge Includes Our Family of Faith

Just as we have a primary responsibility to our immediate families, God has established us in a body of believers or a church family. The following passages from the Bible reveal God's expectations for the body of Christ:

Galatians 6:2 – Carry each other's burdens, and in this way you will fulfill the Law of Christ.

Galatians 6:10 – Therefore, as we have opportunity, let us do good to all people, especially to those who belong to the family of believers.

Acts 2:44-47 – All the believers were together and had everything in common. Selling their possessions and goods, they gave to anyone as he had need. Every day they continued to meet together in the temple courts. They broke bread in their homes and ate together with glad and sincere hearts, praising God and enjoying the favor of all the people. And the Lord added to their number daily, those who were being saved.

Eric Wallace, founder and president of Uniting Church and Home, encouraged us that when our churches rediscover their identity as God's household—a network of integrated living stones not made by human hands; "Then the world will begin to see the witness of God through the church as never before." Gornik wrote; " It is this common life—how people care for one another, generate new patterns of relationship, and take seriously the call to serve their neighbors—that sets the church apart, even more than its building, its programs, its pastor, or its preaching." Wallace observed that; "What has happened in many cases is programs have become the life of the church, taking the place of relationships." We can't love people through programs. We love one another through relationships.

Sometimes, we even need to tell people that they have a responsibility to communicate to us when they have needs. While we have a responsibility to love our neighbors, they have a responsibility to let us know when they need extra love and care. This is how God's community grows; how love is exercised and our gifts identified. Our church family must not hide their needs from each other, yet many do.

Study Questions

1. Does the church have a responsibility to help all of its members and regular attenders? Why? Why not?

2. In what situations would it probably be more appropriate for a church to use other means, outside of itself, to help its members? Are there some means that may not be appropriate to use?

3. Can you name some of the means, outside of what your church provides, that have been used to help members or regular attenders?

4. Who in the church is responsible for making sure its members are being helped?

5. How would you know when someone in the church needs help?

Two Ends to a Bridge — One Anchored in Households

A bridge extends from you to a place where you are going; it makes a connection between you and someone or somewhere else. The end that you are standing on needs attention. Your end must be grounded in a firm foundation. The firmest foundation is a godly household.

Households are basic building blocks. God has blessed nations through households. He uses them, with their leadership, structure, and inheritance, to maintain His kingdom:

> Genesis 18:18-19 – Abraham will surely become a great and powerful nation, and all nations on earth will be blessed through him. For I have chosen him, so that he will direct his children and his household after him to keep the way of the Lord by doing what is right and just, so that the Lord will bring about for Abraham what he has promised him.

Wallace explained that, in Deuteronomy 6, we find; "God's plan accomplished over generations through heart-level relationships that are nurtured in everyday life." The four operative words here are generations, relationships, hearts, and everyday life. Households embody a natural focus on the basic needs of life and on basic care. Welfare, education, self-government, training, food, clothing, shelter, hospitality, personal care, and accountability naturally reside within households.

In addition, Wallace suggested that a godly household offers a natural outreach into the community. Christ-committed households can be awesome instruments used by God for ministry in the neighborhoods where God has planted them. God has done amazing redemptive work through households! But we still need to be cautious not to overcommit to situations that may very well be beyond our capabilities. The council of church leaders and others, through shared experience and training, can help provide protection against this pitfall.

Examples of Creative Ways for Households to be Better Prepared to Cross the Bridges to Show Compassion

Relationship or Bridge	Potential Future Need	Preparation
A friend of your daughter's at school	Uniforms for school	Keep uniforms that your children have outgrown to hand down to other children
Elderly neighbor	Occasionally needs food at the end of the month when social security money runs out	Keep a food reserve; buy an extra can of low salt food every time you go shopping
Co-worker	Occasionally, car repairs are needed so he doesn't lose his job	Teach your co-worker how to do routine maintenance on his car
Homeless person	Shelter during extreme heat or cold	Keep extra bus tokens so he can get to a shelter
Grandmother	Shut-in who becomes isolated during the winter	Save extra food when you make dinner and deliver the extra food weekly

Wallace explained that the home is a natural center of ministry; "Ministry that occurs outside of the home, generally speaking, is ministry that is out of touch with everyday life. . . . Each household has its own complete society, having its own unique culture. Aspects of government, law, charity, justice, and compassion are inherent to any societal structure and are also found within the [household]. Such components enable households to serve in the most dynamic way." Our households can provide a solid anchor to the end of the bridge that starts with us.

Each household represents a number of personal relationships or connections, ever present in the community, every hour of every day. Keller stated that every Christian household can develop its own ministry of mercy by looking at the needs closest to it, and meeting them through loving deeds and a spirit of encouragement. Households can be places for wonderful creativity in finding ways to love our neighbors. Here is one example:

> It was a winter day. The sun was setting. The snow had stopped falling. Before the night came and it got colder I decided to shovel what I could. My wife helped and we cleared our front steps and walkway in a half hour. She went in to make dinner and I proceeded to shovel my neighbor's walkway.
>
> We were new in the neighborhood. It had been difficult to build trust with one of our neighbors. She was retired and lived alone. I felt that shoveling snow would be a way of showing that we wanted to be good neighbors. Perhaps even to provide an example of what love might look like if Jesus were her neighbor. In fact, back-breaking work without an expectation of repayment had always opened doors with our neighbors.

Households, crossing their existing bridges to carry compassion to their neighbors, can be awesome instruments of mercy and the Gospel, especially when supported by the church.

Study Questions

1. Describe some ways in which your household has helped your neighbors.

2. How can children play a role in helping their households minister to their neighbors?

3. Describe some ways in which someone else's household has helped you or your household.

4. What are some of the strengths found in household relationships that create a sense of community and provide practical care?

5. Does the church share some of these strengths, as found in households? Please describe them.

The Role of Leadership

The ministry of compassion or mercy can be done holistically through the church. Keller explained; "The ministry of mercy is the meeting of "felt" needs through deeds. As agents of the kingdom, the church seeks to bring substantial healing of the effects of sin in all areas of life, including psychological, social, economical, and physical." The church has the opportunity to bring healing from the effects of sin on all aspects of life: felt needs, physical needs, psychological needs, social needs, economical needs, and spiritual needs.

It must be clarified, however, that the ordained leaders of the church are not the primary doers of the ministry of mercy. We don't stand back and wave them on as they cross our bridges. Compassion is expected of every citizen of God. However, the leaders of the church are to be encouragers and equippers of God's people. It's their responsibility to see to it that our households are equipped and prepared for crossing our bridges.

The following story shows how a church leader encouraged a household to take the lead in responding to a neighboring family's needs:

It's 10:30 at night and the phone rings.

"Hello."

"Can I speak with Gary?"

"That's me. What's up?"

"My neighbor had a fire yesterday. I was wondering if the Deacons could visit them and see how our church can help out?"

"The fire happened yesterday?"

"Yep."

"It's ten thirty at night."

"Oh, I'm sorry. But they had a fire and they were wandering around their house today collecting what they could."

"Do they live nearby?"

"Yea, two houses down."

"Do they know you?"

"Oh yes. Our children played together for years. We even had them over for dinner once."

"Do they trust you?"

"I would think so after all these years."

"Then how about this idea? Tomorrow, you and your family pay them a visit. Bring some dinner over. Sit and talk with them. Listen to their needs. Then after a time of praying and thinking about what you've heard, have your family come up with some ideas on how we, as a church, through your relationship can help. Can you do that?"

"I guess we can but . . . does that mean the Deacons won't visit them?"

"This is how we will start. We will build on the existing connection between your family and your neighbor's family. They don't know us. They know and trust you. They probably even hope that you will reach out to them, for you said you've known them all these years. Once you assess their needs then we can talk about how our church can support your relationship and help you meet their needs."

The leaders of the church must provide training in discernment to people in the church who want to help others. Fortunately, we do not have to develop the training materials. Others, such as Dr. David Apple, in Philadelphia, with his book, *Not Just a Soup Kitchen*, have already provided a lot of background information for training. However, consider the following cautions as examples of what must be taught:

- Felt needs are only the tip of the iceberg. Once we get involved we often find that deeper issues and needs arise.

- Don't rush into mercy ministry naïve of sin. We often feel manipulated and taken advantage of because even in times of need we sin against one another.

- Few needs are emergencies. People will make their needs appear to be urgent to emphasize the needs and get what they want.

- Pace yourself. Protect against burnout. Establish prayer partners to keep guard over your own welfare.

- Know when to seek experienced advice or refer people to professionals.

Here is one story of how church leaders erred in watching over God's resources when providing help to a man who claimed to be in distress:

> Daryl wandered into the church during worship. A tall and healthy looking man in his 30's, he came seeking help. Another Deacon and I were pulled out of worship to talk with him. I started asking questions. He said he needed $21.75 to add to the money he already had to buy a train ticket to Newark. His wife and daughter had been in New Jersey visiting a sister-in-law who just had a baby and needed help at home. They were on their way home in the only car they owned when they got into an accident with a drunken driver. Both were in the hospital and he had no way of transportation to visit them. He said he's an only son and that his father was deceased and his elderly mother was on assistance—that his wife's family was a mess and would be of no help to him. He gave me an address and a phone number. We got some money together (passed around the hat, so to speak) and sent him off with a younger man from the church to take him to the bus station. The younger man gave Daryl the money when Daryl asked to stop at a house so he could get some belongings for the trip. Daryl ran into the house and never came out.

Discernment is needed. In 1 Timothy 5:3-16, we learn that the church's charity is not indiscriminate. Just because someone has a need does not mean that it is a legitimate claim against God's resources. Also, we might be taken advantage of. We should expect it yet err on the side of mercy as often as possible.

We tend to feel that in order to love our neighbors there must be some reasonable limit to closeness. Can you hear your neighbors when they argue? Does the smoke from their barbecue grill drift through your windows? Do your neighbors use your driveway for overflow parking when they have a weekend party? What limits does God place on being a good neighbor? Robert Frost considered something like this in his poem, *Mending Wall*: "Good fences make good neighbors." Perhaps restated it could be, "Good neighbors respect the fences." Yet God has called us to love our neighbors as well as we love ourselves. Because this can be a hard calling to follow, we often allow this "love" to be placed into programs within the church where it can be controlled. On the contrary, we are to love our neighbors in ways that make little sense to the world around us. Consider how Christ's love for us was demonstrated in a way that still makes no sense to the unbelieving world. Are we not to follow in Jesus' ways?

Examples of Crossing Bridges to Minister Compassion with the Church's Support

Relationship or Bridge	Situation	What Can You Do?	How Can Your Church Help?
Next-door neighbor	House fire	Visit, ask about needs, bring food, pray with him	Pray for him, donate furniture and clothes
Uncle	Lost job	Visit, take him to dinner, pray with him	Pray for him, search for job connections, make meals
Co-Worker	Extended sickness	Visit or call, deliver meals, mow lawn, pray with her	Pray for her, collect money to help pay med. bills, make meals
Child's Teacher	Death of a spouse	Visit, attend the funeral, pray with her	Pray for her, provide a connection to a support group

Study Questions

1. Describe some ways in which your church currently provides help to people who are not members.

2. How can a church over-extend its support to someone and get into trouble? Explain.

3. Who in your church is responsible for making sure that this does not happen?

4. Are there other ways in which your church can provide help to people in your community?

5. Are there people in your church who work in outside organizations and agencies that provide help for people in your community? How might they be of help to your church and its ministries?

Take Home Message

God has called us—as individuals, as households, and as a community—to use the resources He has given us to meet the obvious needs of the people in the existing relationships in which He has already placed us. Some of these relationships bring us joy and result in friendships. Some of these relationships cause frustration and become a concern. Relationships are scary, emotionally draining, are hurtful at times, and require time and energy to maintain. Nonetheless, God is a bridge builder. We are honored that he would build bridges for us to cross so that we can play a role in redeeming His community.

God calls us to love our neighbors. And God places us where we can meet those neighbors. Yet too often we choose the neighbors we want to love—the neighbors that we feel we can relate to or that will show appreciation for our help. And we decide what that love should look like—a love that is convenient and easy to give. But Christ challenges us to love beyond our comfort level; stretching us to the point where faith must step in and take over. Relationships change us. To love our neighbor as ourselves means we need to have a healthy view of who we are; of our brokenness and God's mercy, redemption, and grace. Christ calls us, and re-creates us, to give of ourselves to others and He provides the power from a right relationship with God.

Yet in all of the activity that we will become involved with, we must not forget that loving the Lord our God with all of our hearts, minds, bodies, and souls comes first. We need to be humbled and filled with God's grace so that the love, mercy, and compassion that we share with others come from the Lord.

May the grace of God make loving the Lord your God a mark of who you are, such that acts of loving your neighbor as yourself are evidenced in your everyday life.

References

Apple, D. 2014. *Not Just a Soup Kitchen*. CLC Publications, Fort Washington, PA.

Gornik, M.R. 2002. *To Live in Peace: Biblical Faith and the Changing Inner City*. William B. Eerdman's Publishing Company, Grand Rapids, MI.

Keller, T.J. 1997. *Ministries of Mercy: The Call of the Jericho Road* (2nd edition). P&R Publishing, Phillipsburg, N.J.

Swan, M. and Biebel, D. 2002. *Romancing Your Child's Heart*. Multnomah Publishers, Sisters, OR.

Wallace, E. E. 1999. *Uniting Church and Home: A Blueprint for Rebuilding Church Community*. Solutions for Integrating Church and Home, Lorton, VA.

Additional Reading

Allender, D. and T. Longman III. 1992. *Bold Love*. Navpress, Colorado Springs, CO.

Crabb, L. 1992. *The IBC Approach to Understanding Who We Are and How We Relate*. NavPress, Colorado Springs, CO.

Frazee, R. 2001. *The Connecting Church: Beyond Small Groups to Authentic Community*. Zondervan, Grand Rapids, MI.

Grant, G. 1999. *The Micah Mandate: Balancing the Christian Life*. Cumberland House, Nashville, TN.

Groningen, J.V. 1996. *Changing Times, New Approaches: A Handbook for Deacons*. CRC Publications, Grand Rapids, MI.

Keller, T. J. 1985. *Resources for Deacons: Love Expressed Through Mercy Ministry*. Christian Education & Publications, Lawrenceville, GA.

Linthicum, R. C. 2003. *Transforming Power: Biblical Strategies for Making a Difference in Your Community*. InterVarsity Press, Downers Grove, IL.

Long, J. 2004. *Emerging Hope: A Strategy for Reaching Postmodern Generations*. InterVarsity Press, Downers Grove, IL.

Perkins, J.M. 1993. *Beyond Charity—The Call to Christian Community Development*. Baker Books, Grand Rapids, MI.

Roley, S and Elliott, J.I. 2004. *God's Neighborhood*. InterVarsity Press, Downers Grove, Ill.

Strauch, A. 1992. *The New Testament Deacon: The Church's Minister of Mercy*. Lewis & Roth Publishers, Colorado Springs, CO.

About the Author

Gary A. Burlingame is a board certified environmental scientist, author, and keynote speaker with more than thirty-five years of experience. Gary has also assisted a variety of volunteer, community-based efforts to meet the practical needs of his neighbors, and he authors books under Healthy Life Press to encourage Christians in their everyday life. *Crossing the Bridges God Builds* came together after studying many books about mercy ministry, being involved in compassion-based ministries, and more than ten years of personal experience as a volunteer deacon in his urban church.

Other Healthy Life Press Books by Gary A. Burlingame

Who Me, Pray? Prayer 101: Praying Aloud, for Beginners

My Broken Heart Sings (poetry)

My Faith – My Poetry (poetry)

Because We're Family
(a giveaway to help in sharing your faith with family)

Because We're Friends
(a giveaway to help in sharing your faith with friends)

Richer Descriptions: A Guide to the Human Senses
(a resource for Christian Speakers and Writers)

Our God-Given Senses: A Bible Study on the Human Senses

See www.healthylifepress.com to order any or all of these books.

Healthy Life Press
Books, eBooks, DVDs
Golden, Colorado

A Small, Independent Christian Publisher with a big mission—to help people live healthier lives physically, emotionally, spiritually, and relationally.

For a downloadable PDF catalog of our resources, and access to free sample excerpts from our books, visit: *www.healthylifepress.com*

1-877-331-2766 | *info@healthylifepress.com*

www.ingramcontent.com/pod-product-compliance
Lightning Source LLC
Chambersburg PA
CBHW042000080526
44588CB00021B/2813